Golden Retrievers

by Nico Barnes

www.abdopublishing.com

Published by Abdo Kids, a division of ABDO, P.O. Box 398166, Minneapolis, Minnesota 55439.

Copyright © 2015 by Abdo Consulting Group, Inc. International copyrights reserved in all countries. No part of this book may be reproduced in any form without written permission from the publisher.

Printed in the United States of America, North Mankato, Minnesota.

052014

092014

 THIS BOOK CONTAINS RECYCLED MATERIALS

Photo Credits: Glow Images, Shutterstock, Thinkstock

Production Contributors: Teddy Borth, Jennie Forsberg, Grace Hansen

Design Contributors: Candice Keimig, Laura Rask, Dorothy Toth

Library of Congress Control Number: 2013952552

Cataloging-in-Publication Data

Barnes, Nico.

 Golden retrievers / Nico Barnes.

   p. cm. -- (Dogs)

ISBN 978-1-62970-031-1 (lib. bdg.)

Includes bibliographical references and index.

1. Golden retrievers--Juvenile literature.   I. Title.

636.752--dc23

                    2013952552

Table of Contents

Golden Retrievers

Golden retrievers are playful.

They are also kind and **gentle**.

Golden retrievers have long, soft fur. Their fur is golden.

7

Goldens **shed** a lot! Brushing them once a day will help.

8

9

Goldens have long tails.

They have **floppy** ears.

Smart Dogs

Golden retrievers are very smart. It is easy to teach them new tricks.

13

Goldens are popular **service dogs**. They help people with **disabilities**.

15

Goldens are great hunting dogs. That is what they were **bred** to do.

17

Exercise

Goldens need daily exercise. They like to swim and play fetch.

Family

Golden retrievers are social dogs. They love to be with their human families.

More Facts

- Golden retrievers love the water. Swimming is great for exercise and for fun.

- Golden retrievers can easily get along with other dogs and cats.

- Golden retrievers were first **bred** in Scotland.

Glossary

breed – breeding dogs to make offspring that act and look a specific way.

disability – a person with a physical or mental handicap.

floppy – limp and hanging loosely.

gentle – calm and sweet.

service dog – a dog that is trained to assist people who have disabilities.

shed – hair that naturally falls off an animal's body.

Index

abdokids.com

Use this code to log on to abdokids.com and access crafts, games, videos and more!

Abdo Kids Code:
DGK0311